ANNE
FRANK

❖ *Why They Became Famous* ❖

ANNE FRANK

Lina Tridenti

Illustrated by Gianni Renna

Translated by Stephen Thorne

Silver Burdett Company

ACKNOWLEDGMENTS

We would like to thank Daniel Horn, Department of History, Rutgers University and Craighton Hippenhammer, Cuyahoga County Public Library, Ohio for their guidance and helpful suggestions.

Library of Congress Cataloging in Publication Data

Tridenti, Lina.
  Anne Frank.

  (Why they became famous)
  Translation of: Perchè sono diventati famosi, Anna Frank.
  1. Frank, Anne, 1929–1945 — Juvenile literature.   2. Holocaust, Jewish
(1939–1945) — Netherlands — Amsterdam — Biography — Juvenile literature.
3. Jews — Netherlands — Amsterdam — Biography - Juvenile literature.
4. Amsterdam (Netherlands) — Biography — Juvenile literature.   I. Frank, Anne,
1929–1945. Achterhuis. English.   II. Title.   III. Series.
DS135.N6F73813 1985   940.53'15'03924   84-40403

ISBN 0-382-06857-2
ISBN 0-382-06987-0 (Soft Cover)

© Fabbri Editori S.p.A., Milan 1982
Translated into English by Stephen Thorne for Silver Burdett Company
from Perché Sono Diventati Famosi: Anna Frank
First published in Italy in 1982 by Fabbri Editori S.p.A., Milan

CONTENTS

Anne's Childhood

Anne Frank was born on June 12, 1929 in Frankfurt, Germany. Her father, Otto Frank, was a Jewish businessman. The situation in Germany was difficult for Jewish people living there at that time. The Nazis were coming into power and persecution of the Jews was beginning. Slowly but surely Jewish people were deprived of their civil and political rights, eventually they were even denied their economic rights.

In 1933 the Enabling Act was passed in Germany which prohibited Jews from holding public office. Eventually, threats and acts of violence prevented them from working in any type of professional jobs. Later, in 1935, the persecution of the Jews climaxed with the passage of the Nuremburg Laws, depriving them of virtually all their rights of citizenship.

The Franks were Jewish, and while living in Germany were subject to the Nazi persecutions. In 1933 Otto Frank, his wife, and their two young daughters, Margot and Anne emigrated from Germany to the relative safety of Holland. The Franks settled in Amsterdam where Otto became a partner in the firm of Kohlen and Company, importers of spices and fruit jelly. The Nazis had not yet occupied Holland, and there the family was able to lead a fairly normal life. In spite of all the hardships they had been through they still had affection for each other, faith in the future, and the will to begin again.

About a year had passed since the Franks had left their home in Frankfurt. The news they heard from Germany was alarming, and they feared for their relatives still living there. However, the arrival of Anne's fifth birthday gave them cause for celebration, and the opportunity to forget for awhile the tragic situation in Germany.

On the evening before her fifth birthday Anne ran out of the house into the garden as she did every evening to wait for her father to arrive home from work. She was a happy little girl, spoiled by everyone because she was the youngest child. Leaving Germany had certainly affected her sister Margot much more than it did Anne. Margot was quieter and more introspective. Mr. Frank had remembered his little girl's birthday. On his way home from work he stopped at a bookshop and came out with a brightly wrapped package. When he arrived home, his daughter Anne came up to him merrily.

"Daddy, look at the lovely doll our friend Miep has given me!" Then she spotted the package under his arm and pointed to it excitedly, "Is that for me, too?" she asked, smiling happily.

"Who knows," her father said, picking her up and hugging her tightly. "And how old are you today, my little one?"

"Five! Have you forgotten that I'm a big girl now? At school today the teacher told me I had been good. Come and let me show you my drawing. Then will you tell me a story?"

Anne was a precocious child, quick and eager to learn. She went to the Montessori school with Margot and made good progress at school every day. "Wait just a moment, Anne," her father said. "Let me say hello to Mother and Margot, and then I'll come."

Anne opened her present, which was a book, and put it next to her drawing on the table in the garden. When her father returned, he looked at the drawing, and smiled.

"Well, how clever you were to do such a good drawing! Now I will read you a story." He reached for the book, opened it, and began reading to his daughter.

Five years passed and conditions in Germany grew worse and worse for the Jews still living there. They were now practically denied any kind of social life. Because of her age, Anne's grandmother had chosen to remain in Frankfurt when the rest of the family left for Holland. Now though, she was afraid. After her two sons escaped to America she decided to join the Franks in Amsterdam.

Anne was happy that her grandmother was going to be with them. While they had been separated the old woman had always been remembered with fondness by her family, and was frequently the topic of their conversations. Anne was still very young when they had been separated from her. During the five years that followed both she and Margot had grown, gone to school, and made new friends. Her grandmother's arrival was a source of great joy for everyone, but especially for Anne. She was a tolerant, thoughtful woman who was always ready to help her granddaughter. She knew just the right words to use when she called Anne, and was always patient and understanding with her.

"Anne, shall we talk a little? Why don't you come over here?"

Her grandmother always managed to get Anne out of a bad mood and make her happy again. She was better than anyone else at persuading Anne to do the things she wanted her to do.

"Will you help me to shell these peas? While we work I can tell you how your parents became engaged." Anne just couldn't resist, and her grandmother could tell any story as if it were a fable. She also persuaded Anne to do her homework and forget about games. "Anne, I can't remember what it was you were telling me yesterday about Greece."

"You're a sly one, Granny! You want me to study history, don't you?" They sat down together and helped each other.

One day, Anne found her grandmother in tears. She tried to comfort her.

"What's wrong Grandmother? Are you thinking about aunty and uncle again? They're fine, safe and sound in America."

"I'll never see them again," sobbed her grandmother. "The war has begun. Who knows how it will end?"

"It has started? But how, and where?" Anne asked.

"Get the atlas and find the map of Germany." Then she pointed to Frankfurt. "This was my city, and yours too. You were all born there."

"But Amsterdam is very nice. We like it here!"

"Well, yes," sighed her grandmother, and stroked her granddaughter's head.

"Show me where the war is!" Anne insisted. "Who wanted it?"

"At the moment no one is actually fighting," her granny explained. "But it's as if they are. Hitler has decided to annex to Germany all countries which are inhabited by Germans. He has occupied Austria and invaded Czechoslovakia. Now he's threatening the neighboring states. He wants to build a great and powerful Reich, and all the world is afraid of him."

"But Granny, except the ones you've mentioned, are there any other countries inhabited by Germans that Hitler is claiming for his own?"

"Not yet as far as I know, but who knows what else he's thinking of doing?"

"He'll stop now, just you see."

"Let's hope you're right, my dear," her grandmother concluded.

The German Occupation

Her grandmother's fears soon came true. On September 1, 1939 Anne was listening to the radio and heard reports that the Germans had moved into Polish territory. Hitler's army had swiftly and forcefully attacked Poland, invading from both land and air. The Polish army fought heroically, but was unable to defend itself for very long against such a formidable invasion. After a month of fighting Poland surrendered to the Germans. Britain and France were now drawn into the war, but before they could organize their forces to provide any assistance, Poland had fallen.

Seven months later, the Germans moved into Scandinavia. Finland fell in March of 1940, and by early June, Denmark and Norway were occupied.

The Germans then turned their attention to France. Luxembourg, Holland, and Belgium lay in their way. On May 14, 1940 Holland surrendered. Hitler's army pressed forward and by the end of June the triumphant Germans entered and occupied Paris, meeting with little resistance after the breakthrough in the north.

The Franks, and other Jewish refugees living in Holland, were now in German occupied territory. Once again they were subject to the laws which authorized discrimination against and persecution of the Jews. Each day there seemed to be more and more laws restricting their lives. And no form of violence was spared in enforcing those laws.

Mr. Frank tried not to discuss the situation when the girls and their grandmother were present. He saw no reason to alarm them. But the subject of persecutions could not always be avoided, and when his friends from work, Mr. Van Daan, Mr Kraler, and Mr. Koophuis came to visit, the topic was always discussed. One evening Mr. Kraler was furious,

"Have you heard what is happening in Germany now?" he shouted. "The Nazis are not just breaking windows, looting shops, and setting fire to houses. They've started going after the synagogues and cemeteries."

"Will it happen here, too?" asked Mrs. Frank.

"No, no, it's different here," her husband reassured her. "They're just passing through Holland to get to France."

"Mr. Van Daan disagreed. "We mustn't deceive ourselves," he said. "The concentration camps have been taking Jews since 1933."

"They must have been Jewish dissenters," asserted Mr. Koophuis.

"No," insisted Van Daan, "they've got it in for the Jews simply because they *are* Jews."

"Yes, but it's not as if we've got 'Jew' written on our foreheads!" said Mr. Frank.

"I know, but we must acknowledge the fact that we are Jews by wearing the yellow Star of David sewn on our clothes—Hitler has ordered it!" Van Daan said with disgust.

"My friends," said Mr. Frank, "why don't we try to do something useful?" The men went away and talked for a long while in secret.

"We must find a safe hiding place," Mr. Frank announced.

Mr. Van Daan shook his head, "There's no way out for us, we'll end up in the concentration camps."

"Unfortunately, that news seems reliable," confirmed Mr. Frank, "and we must face the facts. We already know that Jews living in other countries occupied by the Germans have suffered at the hands of the Nazis."

In spite of the war, daily life still went on quite normally, but the German occupation could be felt continually. The Frank family received the sad news that some of their friends had been subjected to persecution, and deported by the Germans. The situation distressed Anne's grandmother greatly and had caused her to age rapidly.

One fine Sunday in the spring Anne was feeling restless. She wandered from room to room and didn't feel at all like studying.

"Daddy, can we go out? Let's go for a walk in town."

"Do you want to go out as well, Margot?" her father asked.

"I ought to study," his other daughter replied.'

"Well you stay at home, then. You can keep grandmother company."

The city of Amsterdam was marvelous in the bright sunshine. In the flowerbeds that lined the walkways, red and yellow tulips were in bloom. It seemed to be a peaceful Sunday—people were strolling along, talking, and stopping in the squares.

"Let's not go too far, we're on foot, you know," Mr. Frank reminded Anne.

"I won't get tired. It's no great hardship to do without the tram on a day as beautiful as this, is it?" Anne was very happy.

"How are things going at school? What does old Mr. Keptor have to say to you?"

"It's better than I thought. I'm not very fond of mathematics, and he has realized it."

"Has he punished you again?"

"I think he has resigned himself to putting up with my talking in class. So far he has given me three essays to write as punishment."

"On what?"

" 'A Chatterbox', 'The Incurable Chatterbox' and...well, the third one is even more stupid." Anne stopped.

"Come on, tell me what it is!" Her father was amused.

" 'Quack, Quack, Quack said Little Miss Goose'," murmured Anne.

"Were you annoyed?"

"He wanted to poke fun at me, but I really showed him!" exploded Anne. "I wrote a fantastic poem with my friend Sanne. Do you like Amsterdam, Daddy?" asked Anne, changing the subject.

"Yes, it's a wonderful city."

"For centuries it was the greatest metropolis in the world," Anne added. "They taught me about it in school."

"It's a pity it's no longer a free city." Mr. Frank sighed.

So Many Things are Forbidden

Anne could easily imagine what her father was thinking about as they walked around the city. They passed by a park and saw a large notice posted in a prominent position. It said that Jews were forbidden to enter the park which was reserved for others.

"So many things are forbidden!" exclaimed Anne.

"It seems that almost every day now there are new anti-Jewish laws forcing us to wear the identification star, forbidding us to use the trams, making us turn in our bicycles, and ordering us not to use our cars..."

"But why?"

"So that we can't avoid their constant scrutiny."

Anne wanted to change the subject. "Shall we buy a cake for Mother?"

"It isn't allowed. We can only do our shopping in authorized Jewish shops from three to five in the afternoon."

"And we can't play sports, we can't go to the movies or the theater, we can't walk in the park or meet people," Anne exclaimed. "What *are* we allowed to do?"

"Be together, at least for the moment. It's already quite something that we are allowed to return to our home."

"Daddy, why do the Germans hate us so much?"

"It's a long story. Palestine was conquered by the Romans in 66 B.C. When the Emperor Hadrian gave Jerusalem the new name of Aelina Capitolina, Bar Kochba, the Hebrew, rebelled. The rebellion failed and from then on Jews were forbidden to re-enter Jerusalem. That was the beginning of the 'diaspora', the dispersal of the Jews. But wherever they were in the world, the Jews remained true to their faith and the synagogue which symbolized continuity and tradition. The exiles always encountered serious problems. The need to survive turned them into expert businessmen in the countries that accepted them, and they were hated for it. They were always persecuted. Aside from now, the worst period was in the Middle Ages, during the time of the Crusades. They were forced into isolation, into 'ghettoes', and excluded from holding public office."

"They never knew peace, then," Anne sighed.

"Only when a king or another ruler used the Jews who were most familiar with economics to sort out the country's finances."

"Why did they nearly always choose trade and business?"

"It's a way of life that creates customs, habits, and choices. The uncertainty of their situation made the Jews realize that it would be better not to own property. Exile forced them to invest in moveable goods. Moneylending was practiced by the Jews because Christians were forbidden to do it."

When the occupation of Holland first began it seemed that the Germans wanted to be agreeable. They tried to win the good faith and collaboration of the people. As soon as the first signs of dissent and resistance appeared, however, they changed their tactics. At first there were threats, followed by reprisals that became harsher as time passed. In September of 1941, General Keitel issued orders to the effect that any action taken against the Nazi occupation forces would result in the immediate shooting of hostages—people who had been imprisoned in order to ensure the submission of the occupied country.

In Amsterdam the severity of the racial laws was felt by the Jewish residents. When the headmistress of the Montessori school came into class one morning to teach 6B its last lesson of the year, Anne knew that for her it was not only the last lesson of the year, but also the last lesson she would ever have at that school. When the lesson ended, she heard the headmistress say,

"I have some sad news for you—we are going to lose one of our pupils, Anne Frank. She has to go to another school next year, and we would all like to wish her well."

Everyone in the class watched as Anne stood up and went to the teacher's desk. "Where are you going?" came a voice from the general murmur that followed her.

"To the Jewish Secondary School," Anne replied immediately in a clear voice.

"But why?" her classmates asked.

"Because the occupation laws say that she must," explained the headmistress.

The pupils where shocked and dismayed. The headmistress held out her hand to Anne, and drew her towards her affectionately, "We have been together for many years. You were a little girl when you first came here in 1934. You have grown up here and we would have liked you to continue your studies with us. It is no longer possible though. We won't forget you." Turning to the class, she added, "History is teaching us a hard lesson."

Her words fell on the stunned silence of the classroom. Anne bowed her head and wept, while the teacher and pupils made no secret of their feelings either.

"Come along, Margot is waiting for you." The headmistress hugged her when they reached the door. "Goodbye, Anne." There was nothing else to say.

Her sister was waiting for her at the entrance with tears in her eyes. They took each other's hands and walked sadly home.

It was the beginning of vacation time but there was little joy in the occasion. The girls had begun to learn, at their own expense, that many of the painful things in life are caused by other human beings.

When vacation ended they entered the Jewish Secondary School they now had to attend. They were happy there. The teachers were good and their new friends were very nice. Anne had some problems with algebra, but her other subjects went very well. Margot did well, too, getting good marks in everything she studied. And so, another term at school came and went without anything unusual happening. Life went on as normally and happily as possible under the circumstances. The death of Anne's grandmother in January 1942 left the family feeling a great sense of emptiness.

A Diary for Anne

It was almost seven o'clock in the morning, but Anne had already been awake for quite awhile. It was June 12, 1942, the day of her thirteenth birthday. She quietly left her bedroom and met their cat, who greeted her with its usual meows and contented purrings.

"How smart you are, Moortje! You want to be the first one to wish me many happy returns of the day!" Bending down, she stroked the cat and picked him up. Then she went down the hall and knocked on the door of her parent's bedroom.

"Happy birthday, Anne!" They hugged her in turn and followed her into the living room to watch her reaction to the presents which were waiting for her there. Anne ran over to the table joyfully.

"Look at all these presents! And so many flowers! And there are even cakes and books, too! Thank you all very much!" Margot appeared in the doorway, barely awake and still in her nightdress, and wished her sister a happy birthday.

"Come on!" suggested her mother. "Open your presents!"

"Shall I start with the smallest? It feels like a book."

"You shouldn't say it—at least try to pretend to be surprised," her sister complained.

"I was wrong! It's a puzzle! How lovely!"

"Do you like it?" asked Margot.

Anne nodded, "Oh yes! And look, here's an envelope with some florins inside. That's good, now I can buy 'The Myths of Greece and Rome'."

Mr. and Mrs. Frank and Margot sat down to enjoy Anne's happiness as she weighed the parcels in her hands, looked at them, and opened them carefully so as not to damage the pretty flowered wrapping paper and the ribbons.

"Your friends have spoiled you today, too," commented her father with a smile.

"They all want to make me read. And look how many lovely flowers there are! Thank goodness I love flowers!" She started unwrapping another parcel.

"A diary!" she cried out. "How marvelous!" she examined the book, rubbed its cardboard cover and held it to her chest. She ran to embrace her father.

"It's my first diary! I'll start writing in it right away, and woe to anyone who tries to read it! I'm going to write all my secrets in it!"

Anne was a spirited, sensitive girl with an extraordinary capacity for grasping the reality of things. She adapted to the fact that she was Jewish and coped with all that it meant. She had made friends at her new school quickly and easily. At her school desk and in her studies she managed to put aside the fact that Holland was an occupied country and a war was going on. She didn't want to use her diary as a self-pitying way of giving release to her feelings, and she didn't want it to be an ordinary account of her day to day life either. She found that she had no special friend, there was not one she could tell everything to.

"What a good idea!" she thought to herself with satisfaction. "My diary will be an imaginary friend for me—I'll tell her everything by writing letters to her!" In fact, it turned out to be a very intimate conversation, fiction and yet not fiction. Her friend was to be called "Kitty".

As time passed the German repression of the Jews grew increasingly harsh. Anne's father had been forced to leave his position at Kohlen and Company—Jews were forbidden to work in business. His Christian friends Koophuis and Kraler carried on for him. It was very sad to watch him brooding silently with no work to do to keep him busy. Fortunately, it was vacation time. His daughters out of school and able to keep him company. One morning, while out walking with Anne, he confided in her.

"You know, we have been entrusting some of our valuables to our Christian friends. We don't want our things to be seized by the Germans and we don't want to be taken away by them either. The day may soon come when we will have to go into hiding. I've been preparing for that possibility for some time now."

"When will we have to go Daddy?" said Anne, unable to hide her anxiety.

"Don't worry, dear." He tried to reassure her. "Just enjoy your vacation."

The following Sunday, July 5, Margot was summoned by the Nazi authorities. She was to present herself at their local headquarters the next day, for deportation. Anne burst into tears when she heard. "It's true, then. They take away young girls alone like this."

"She isn't going!" Mrs. Frank said decisively. "Come on, grab what you can and stick it in your bags. We are going to run away."

Anne ran from place to place putting her favorite things into her school bag. She was careful to pack her diary before anything else. When her father arrived home he went to call his friends. His secretary, Miep, who had just gotten married, came by with her husband, Henk Van Santen. The couple filled their bags and pockets with whatever there was to be taken away and made two trips to the hiding-place.

On Monday morning Mrs. Frank woke the children up at five-thirty. Since any Jew seen walking about with a suitcase would have aroused suspicion she had the children put on many layers of clothing.

"Wear as many clothes as you can, one on top of the other. Come on, be quick!" Fortunately the weather was cool and rainy so it did not look that strange for them to be wearing coats in the summer.

Margot, burdened down with a satchel full of books, was the first to leave on her bicycle. Miep, who had very generously returned to help them, went with her. Moortje the cat prowled restlessly from room to room. Anne petted him silently.

"What about Moortje?" she asked in a sobbing voice.

"I've thought about him, too. Mr. Goudsmit can look after him. He'll be fine—he can stay here in his own home."

At seven o'clock, after embracing and kissing her cat, Anne went around the house saying goodbye to the rooms with her eyes, and then left with her parents.

The street was beginning to come to life. There were mainly workmen about, and they looked at the Franks with compassion. They touched their caps ever so slightly, perhaps in greeting, to show that they understood what it must be like to be a Jew in German held territory. The Franks walked in silence, pretending to be unconcerned. After awhile, Anne realized that they had come through the back streets to the Prinsengracht Canal. She was surprised when she saw the building they had come to.

"But father, do you mean that we are going to hide in your office?"

"It will be a good hiding place, just wait and see! I've been preparing it for some time now. I had planned for us to come here on July 16th, but because the Nazis have summoned Margot we've had to come sooner. Our rooms are not as prepared as I would have liked, but everything will work out."

Life In Hiding

The offices of Kohlen & Co. were in an old four-story building. After passing through corridors and storerooms and going up and down stairs they arrived at the rooms, divided between two floors, where they were to live in secret.

When Anne arrived at the hiding place Margot and Miep were already at work, cleaning and putting things in order. Mrs. Frank sat and said nothing. Everything had happened so quickly that she still hadn't been able to take in the great change that had occurred in their lives. There wasn't much space, but everyone felt lucky to be safe and near friends like Miep, Mr. Krahler, and Mr. Koophuis who all worked downstairs.

Later, on July 13, they were to be joined by their friends the Van Daans and their fifteen-year-old son Peter. Mr. Van Daan had worked with Otto Frank. In November they were joined by an eighth refugee, a dentist named Mr. Dussel.

As the days passed the refugees organized their lives together, and worked out regulations and schedules so they would not arouse the suspicions of the people working in the offices below. They quickly discovered just how difficult it can be to live with other people, shut away for months without being able to go out of doors, and closed in on all sides. Everyone had their jobs to do—cleaning, cooking, reading, studying, and repaying the generosity of their protectors by doing office work like accounting, filing, and correspondence.

Every so often there was some good news over the radio that revived their hopes. In the evening Anne was free to do as she pleased. For awhile she amused herself by watching the last of the birds flying about. Then, when night fell and the lights were out, she took out her telescope and spied on the world outside.

In spite of the war and the suffering that people had unleashed upon one another, the seasons continued to change as always. Nature followed its usual course, and the roses in the street below the window grew and bloomed.

"Oh, if only I could go out to run in the street, and breathe some fresh air!" Anne confided to Peter. He was almost always silent about such things. "Come here, look and see how beautiful the roofs in Amsterdam are. I'd like to go for a ride on a bicycle, or dance—anything just so I could feel young and free. Instead, all I can do is breathe fresh air through a little crack in a window. It makes me feel like crying."

Peter looked at her sympathetically but could think of nothing to say that might comfort her.

It was difficult for everyone to get along while living together in the secret hiding place. Getting along harmoniously in such a confined space would have been difficult under even the best of circumstances. But the refugees also had to cope with the constant fear of discovery by the Nazi authorities. This only added to the already tense atmosphere.

The young people often found the conversations the adults had boring and unimaginative. They seemed to do nothing but complain about everything from food to politics and dwell upon any mistakes the children made.

"Margot really is virtue personified," said Anne. "She's quiet, busy, tidy, faultless, and pretty—she does everything perfectly!"

"You wouldn't be jealous, would you?" laughed Peter.

"No, no—I like Margot, but I can't stand the way they're always scolding me."

During the period in hiding Anne had changed quite a bit. She had grown more mature, yet she was still a bright and precocious young girl. She was keenly self-critical, and suffered all the doubts and questionings of adolescence. As she tried to assert and affirm her own identity she found herself in constant opposition with the adults. She passed much of her time quietly, frequently escaping into day dreams, or letting her feelings out by writing in her diary. It became an outlet for all those feelings pent up inside of her. Day after day she kept a daily record of the things that went on around her and inside of her.

Lately, Peter had been friendlier and the two had grown closer to each other. He, too, was arguing with his parents more frequently, especially with his mother, who was a vain, superficial woman.

One day, Anne had gone to get some potatoes. She stopped for a moment, and asked him what he was studying.

"I'm doing some French exercises," he answered.

"Can I see your translation?"

"Yes, do. You're much smarter than I am anyway."

"What will you do when the war is over?"

"I'll go live on a plantation in the Dutch West Indies."

"Why so far way?"

"I don't think I will have anything better to choose. What about you?"

"I want to be a writer, but first I'll have to study hard. Peter, why do you think so little of yourself? I think you underestimate yourself too much, you know."

"Perhaps, but on the other hand, I don't have much to boast about."

"Why do you say that? Your English is very good, you're brave, and you're also nice looking. We're always fighting with the grown-ups here, and feeling sad, but when this nightmare is over our lives will be very different. Why don't we help each other and be friends. We both need someone to talk to."

"I'd like to be able to talk with you very much."

"We can study together and discuss all kinds of things, can't we?"

"Yes, I'd like that."

"At least we can help each other get things off our chests." Anne suggested. "It would be quite a relief, don't you think?"

"You've already helped me a lot."

"Really? How?"

"Just by being so light-hearted and cheerful." Peter touched her hand.

"I have things to do now," said Anne, hurriedly. "Otherwise there'll be no potatoes for dinner." She was happy now that she had a friend so close by.

For the eight refugees, the hardest part of living in hiding was not being deprived of their freedom, nor the isolation and fear of discovery. It was the endless number of small, daily deprivations and annoyances which they resigned themselves to, suffering silently. The only thing that made it bearable was the faint, fragile hope that they would manage to avoid capture.

One of the biggest problems they had to deal with was food, which they all needed simply to survive. Before fleeing, Mr. Frank and Mr. Van Daan had bought large sacks of beans and potatoes, many cans of vegetables, and some preserved meat on the black market. But the war was lasting much longer than they had expected and in spite of their frugality their supply of food was getting low. By a stroke of luck though, their friends were managing to work miracles. They succeeded in acquiring some extra ration cards and were able to risk buying food for the refugees from their acquaintances.

The kitchen was run on food cycles. At present it was potatoes and beets, there had also been the endive, spinach, turnip, cucumber, cabbage, and tomato periods. Day after day they had the same thing for lunch and dinner, cooked in a different way, sometimes. When this went on for any length of time, there were outbursts of bad temper at the table which led to ugly scenes.

Margot was the only one who never got involved and ate very little. On the other hand Mrs. Van Daan seemed to always be in the thick of it.

"The vegetables aren't bad, thank heavens, and they are good for you. Margot is too pale. She doesn't eat enough."

"At least she doesn't waste any," replied Anne, annoyed, "considering the fact that some of us eat more than our share."

"What impertinence!" burst out Mrs. Van Daan. "What are you trying to say?" Pointless arguing followed, along with criticisms that resulted in long faces.

When they weren't fighting, the Van Daans, as overbearing and meddlesome as they were, did try to create a jovial atmosphere. Mr. Van Daan was incapable of being quiet—he knew everything, spoke about everything. At meals his wife always served him first, giving him the best bits of food. Strong from working in the kitchen, Mrs. Van Daan never missed an opportunity to show off her wisdom and charm. She was a vivacious woman but was also a gossip and could always find a way to provoke an argument between Anne and her mother.

Mrs. Frank worked hard, too, tidying up and doing the washing. She never wasted time with idle chatter. Mr. Frank was a good-hearted man who always tried to stay calm. Before serving himself he would always ask if the children had enough.

The refugees had to follow a rigid schedule so as to avoid being heard by the office workers downstairs. Breakfast—dry bread and margarine—was at nine o'clock and dinner was at one. They had supper when offices were deserted in the evening. Miep, Elli, Mr. Kraler, and Mr. Koophuis often joined them to eat and discuss the BBC (British Broadcasting Corporation) news broadcasts together.

Sometimes there were happy moments when everyone found the energy to smile and be more pleasant. Anne was the youngest and by far the most spirited. She always managed to make jokes and be light-hearted when they were all seated around the table cleaning vegetables, peeling the potatoes, shelling the peas, or separating the good beans from the moldy ones.

There were celebrations, too, and birthday parties when small gifts, greeting cards, and little poems were exchanged.

Now and then, someone would come out with, "Someday we will all look back on this time..."

Anne had a rich imagination and had found many ways to keep herself from getting bored. One way she amused herself was by doing dance steps to stay nimble. Her mother's birthday was coming up shortly and she wanted to liven up the celebration with a ballet dedicated to her. She had already made herself a costume from an old camisole and had decorated it with ribbons. Mr. Kraler had brought some sugar so they were able to make a cake. All of this made Mrs. Van Daan green with envy.

As everyone reached the limits of their tolerance arguments over the smallest things came more frequently. It was almost impossible to live in that way for as long as they had. They were cut off from the rest of the world, always fearful of capture and death, completely dependent on the help of their friends who ran the risk of terrible punishment if they were caught.

Another year came and went, it was now 1944 and they had been in hiding for 19 months. Relations between Anne and her family had deteriorated greatly. Things were particularly difficult with her mother and Anne vowed to herself that she would never be like her.

"If God lets me live through this," she thought, "I'll do things that my mother has never done. I'll never resign myself to being an ordinary woman the way she has! I'll work in the big world for other people!" Like many young people, Anne was a mass of contradictions. Her father and Margot tried to help her understand her mother's situation a little better.

"Mother used to be rich, you know, and she didn't have all the problems she has now. All these economies, sacrifices, and fears have certainly changed her a lot. How can you expect her to be happy and easy-going, poor soul?"

Even under normal circumstances, adolescence is a difficult period, but in the situation in which they found themselves Anne, Peter, and Margot all found it practically unbearable. As if their parents weren't enough, there was also Mr. Dussel who never missed an opportunity to point out everything that was wrong or inappropriate.

Mr. Frank was a kind man, but he couldn't give Anne the things she was missing. In order to develop her own identity and independence she needed to break away from her family, to have new experiences, and get to know the world and other people. The hiding, the isolation, and the overcrowding made everything so much more difficult for her.

In her diary she wrote: "I realize that when I came here in 1942 I was an impertinent, spoiled little girl, sincere but not realistic. That time is over now. Life was all smiles before, but now all that has changed, too. There are arguments and criticisms. The truth is that I have grown..."

Sometimes she was overcome with sadness. She felt lonely, treated unfairly, and at odds with everyone. At other times, she felt confident, contented, and warm towards everyone. Then she would wonder how she could have been so harsh and critical in her judgement of her mother, hurting her so and making her cry. She searched inside herself to find the reason for her behavior. To her it all seemed terribly serious.

Anne had truly grown. She had learned to see people and things as they really were. Each day she shared the pain of millions of men, women, and children and felt along

Anne had truly grown. She had learned to see people and things as they really were. Each day she shared the pain of millions of men, women, and children and felt along with them the harsh realities of war. She was frightened for herself, her family, and her friends. Yet in spite of everything she still managed to love and have hope for a time when life would be good again and peace would return.

At half past nine on the evening of Easter Sunday, 1944, Peter called Mr. Frank and asked him for some help translating a passage from English.

Peter hadn't wanted to alarm anyone, but the fact was that he had heard someone trying to force open the door to the warehouse. It wasn't the first time. Kohlen & Company had often been visited by thieves and each time it happened the fear of discovery grew worse among the refugees. The long imprisonment had been exhausting and everyone had become tense and jumpy.

The girls were sent up to the Van Daans with their mother while the men went downstairs to wait. They heard a loud noise. All the lights were out. Peter summoned up his courage and crept downstairs to try to see what was happening. The revolving bookcase that hid the entrance to their hiding place was ajar and he was able to see the storeroom door. A panel had been broken and the thieves were trying to widen the hole so that they could get into the room. Peter made a sign and Mr. Van Daan suddenly cried out with all his might, "Police, Police!"

The thieves fled and the men in the hiding place tried to put the panel back on the front door, but someone dropped it outside.

There was a couple passing by outside. They looked inside the room with a flashlight. The men had no choice but to pretend that they were the thieves themselves!

"Now those people will certainly call the police!" said Peter.

"What can we do?" asked Mr. Dussel.

"It's a holiday today," Mr. Frank answered. "No one will be at work here for the next two days. Will we have to live in fear of a search for all that time?"

"Hide the radio," said Mrs. Van Daan. "If they discover it, goodbye!"

"They will find Anne's diary," her mother said.

"We should burn it," someone said.

"Not my diary! No!" Anne protested.

"Let's not talk nonsense!" interrupted Mr. Frank. "If they find us, the fact that we're Jewish is enough. We should stop thinking about the worst that could happen. We must try to be brave!"

The night seemed endless. They passed it in a silence broken only by an occasional sigh. The fright had given everyone dysentery which had created another problem because no one could go down to empty the emergency chamber pot. Finally at seven in the morning, they telephoned Mr. Koophuis from the office telephone to let him know what had happened.

Using the excuse of taking food to the warehouse cat, Elli, Miep, and Henk arrived and told the refugees what had happened. The night-watchman had alerted the police. Henk said that he had made a statement to the police and tried to minimize what had happened to draw suspicion away from the hiding-place. In order to avoid a search he even said that nothing had been stolen. It seems that the couple who had looked into the room were a fruit vendor and his wife who lived in the neighborhood.

"He must already have his suspicions," said Miep, "but we're sure he won't talk."

"We've managed to escape the worst once again!" they all thought with relief.

So the worst had passed, but it was not easy to get over the fear of that night. Everyone was left with feelings of great weariness and painful uncertainty.

Anne Looks to the Future

It was a warm sunny day, one of those days when all you want to do is go out and enjoy the fine weather. But of course, no one in the hiding place could go out of doors. All they could do was imagine the things they might have been doing had their situation been different. Days like this made it especially difficult for Anne and the others to be in hiding.

"When will we ever be able to just go outside and enjoy the fine weather whenever we want?" Anne asked her father.

"The news of the war seems good," he replied. "The Allies are making progress, things should get better soon."

"Yes, but even so, now anti-Semitism is spreading everywhere," complained Mr. Van Daan bitterly. "People blame the Jews for everything."

"That's the fault of the Nazis," insisted Mr. Frank. "They persecute anyone who tries to help us. Any act of resistance or assistance unleashes all the cruelty the Germans are capable of."

"Father," Anne asked, "Holland welcomed us when we came here as refugees, but now that the country has been occupied by the Nazis the Dutch have turned their backs on us. Will they make us leave here when the war is over? I've grown up here, and now Holland is more a home to me than Germany."

"We shouldn't listen to rumors," Mr. Frank said. "Let's think about how good things will be when peace comes."

"What would you all like to do when we get out of here?" asked Peter, trying to change the subject.

"I'd like to have a real bath with hot water!" Margot burst out.

"Me too!" added Mrs. Van Daan. "A long, long bath!"

"I want to look for Lotte, my wife," said Mr. Dussel sadly.

"Anne, what would you like to do most of all?" Peter insisted.

"It's hard to say what I would like to do the most," Anne replied. "All I know is that I want to live in my own house, I want my freedom back, and I want to be able to return to my old school and see all my friends. It doesn't matter whether or not I'm Jewish, I'm still just a young girl who wants to lead a normal life. I just need to be happy and have some fun."

Mrs. Van Daan was touched by what Anne had said, "You are right, Anne my dear. This nightmare will be over shortly. I'm sure the Allies will invade the continent soon. Then it won't be long before we can leave this place and lead normal lives again."

Her husband contradicted her and the two began to argue. Everyone else returned to their various tasks and tried to ignore their squabbling. Peter pursued his question with Anne who was quite willing to discuss her dreams for the future.

"What would you like to do with your life when this is all over?"

"Study, grow up, find an exciting job, work hard—I have so much to learn. I'd love to spend a year in Paris or London studying languages and art history. I'd like to travel and see the world, just do all kinds of things."

"So many plans. I almost envy you!"

"Envy me! Why? Don't you ever dream of anything? I have so many dreams that I

would like to make come true. I just hope I'll be able to. After the war I'd like to write a book about all that has happened to me here during the war. I want to be famous, I want to leave something behind when I die."

"Keep talking Anne, I'm enjoying this."

"If you won't laugh at me, I'll tell you about some of the things I've written in my diary."

"Why should I laugh at you?"

"Well, just listen to me then. I'm young and I'm going through this unique experience. I can't spend the days complaining just because I have to live this way. I can feel my mind maturing as the days pass. I believe that nature is beautiful, that there are good people around me, and that freedom is getting closer. Why should I let myself be sad and melancholy and lose hope for the future?"

Peter looked at her with admiration, "Oh Anne, how brave and strong you are, I wish we could all feel more like you!"

That evening the air-raid sirens had sounded their warning. The people of Amsterdam went to take cover. Many people hid in air-raid shelters, but the eight refugees could

not leave their secret hiding place. Anxiously they waited, hoping the signal might be a false alarm. But when the roar of the planes grew louder and louder they knew another spell of bombing was about to begin. Then all they could do was pray that the warehouse building they were hiding in would not be hit, and they would be spared.

Fire from the anti-aircraft guns increased. The noise they made mingled with the sounds of the exploding bombs dropped from Allied aircraft. The aerial bombardment was terrifying. The whistling noise of the bombs dropping, the roar and vibration of the explosions, and the glare from the flames scared everyone. The sky darkened, the house shook, and the windows seemed to shatter into thousands of pieces. What would happen to them if the building they were hiding in was hit? Where would they go?

Anne couldn't stand the bombings and was often on the verge of crying out with fear. She clung to her parents and they held her and tried to provide what little comfort they could.

"Daddy, light a candle, please light a candle!"

"You know I can't. Please, try and be brave Anne."

"I feel so afraid in the dark!"

Mrs. Frank took pity on her daughter and ran to light the candle. The light made them all feel somewhat safer. Ann clutched her little suitcase, ready to flee if a bomb hit and it suddenly became necessary to evacuate the building. She was not the only one who was afraid of the bombs. Everyone in the hiding place was, and no one tried to conceal their feelings. They all tried to think about other things so they would not notice the wail of the sirens and ignore the fact that they were living in the midst of such a terrible ordeal.

By the middle of July, 1944, much of Amsterdam was in ruins. There were too many

dead to count anymore, and the hospitals were filled with wounded. Survivors wandered amidst the smoking ruins, desperate, and just barely aware of what was going on around them. At the end of July there was another day of terrible bombing. The alarm first sounded during breakfast, and once again at around two o'clock. Another warning came in the evening at dinnertime. They had barely had time to recover from one bout of terror, when the sirens announced that the next one was on its way. Airplanes crowded the sky, and with their engines screaming unleashed many tons of bombs on the city. In the glare of the flames Amsterdam seemed to be a mass of holes and craters. When the flames died down the city disappeared from view.

Earlier, on the twenty-fifth day of May, the man who owned the fruit and vegetable market just up the street from the refuge had been arrested by the Germans. He had been hiding two Jews in his home. When this news had reached those living in the refuge it frightened them terribly, giving them even more to worry over. Since then, they not only feared for themselves, but also for their friends who had been protecting them for so long. They were all on the verge of giving in to the tiredness and desperation they felt so intensely.

The heat of the summer was soon upon them. Food was scarce, and much of what they did have was spoiled. The sewers were blocked, and water was not drinkable. The two years had been long ones for Miep, Mr. Kraler, and Mr. Koophuis, too. Seeing to the needs of the eight refugees took up a good deal of their time and energy every day.

Something was making everyone tense. It was more than tiredness, fear of capture, hunger, or the desire for freedom. There was a feeling of expectancy in the air that weighed heavily on all of them. Conversation came and went, moods changed quickly, and the tension increased. They thought they heard unusual noises and footfalls in the warehouse. Had someone discovered their secret hiding place? Or was someone trying to confirm the suspicion that there was one?

One evening, just around midnight, Mr. Frank said, "There's someone there! I'm sure of it!" The Van Daans, who were upstairs, had heard the same noise. Everyone eventually went to sleep, fearful of even the slightest noise. Periodically throughout the night they all got up and listened anxiously. There was someone loitering near the revolving bookcase that led up to the refuge, the noise was unmistakable.

The same thought was running through each person's head, "Who could be poking around out there?"

Most likely it was someone who hated Jews and wanted to earn the bounty money that the Germans had promised to Dutch informers—five gulden (about $1.40) for each Jew reported to the authorities. Miep and Ellie and other friends had always been very cautious, but lately they had felt that one of the men who worked in the storeroom suspected something.

"He's always hanging around on the street by the entrance to the warehouse, pretending to be doing something to his bicycle. He watches our movements suspiciously," Elli had observed.

"He seems to be very curious. He's no fool, and I just don't trust him at all," was Kraler's observation.

"It's no surprise though," Miep had explained. "The war has changed everyone. Even children have learned how to hate. People only look out for themselves now, even if it means doing harm to others."

Anne's Life in Hiding Comes to an End

On the morning of August 4, 1944 everyone in the refuge awoke as usual at a quarter past seven. One by one they took turns going to wash and relieve themselves. The street outside began to come to life. The voices and noises of people starting work for the day could be heard.

Four men in raincoats were walking along the Prinsengracht Canal. They looked like the police. Another man, about forty years old, stood smoking a cigar on the pavement outside the offices of Kohlen and Company where the hiding place was. When the other four reached him he nodded and said, "This is the place!" After a moment they entered the old building together. Mr. Kraler was in his office.

"I am a Gestapo officer," announced one of the men.

"We wish to search the warehouses," added another who, like his companions, was armed, and dressed in the uniform of the Dutch Nazi Police.

Kraler showed them around the building. They examined everything intently as they walked about. When it seemed that the visit was nearly over, Kraler began to relax a little and hope that just maybe everything would be all right. But then the officer continued on down the corridor. When he reached the end where the revolving bookcase was he stopped and ordered Kraler to open it.

"How can I open it, it's just a bookcase!" Kraler protested.

The officers took out their pistols while their leader, pushing Kraler to one side, wrenched at the bookcase. It turned on its hinges to reveal the hidden door.

"Open it!" he ordered. When it was opened he waved his pistol, motioning for Kraler to go up the stairs. The officer pushed his pistol into Kraler's back. Mrs. Frank, seated at the table, was paralyzed with fear as she watched them coming up the stairs. The Van Daans and Franks appeared and stood in a line.

"Hands up!" snapped the officer. The eight Jews obeyed in stunned silence.

"You are coming with us, you have five minutes to pack some clothes."

Meanwhile, the other police officers were searching the premises. The chief officer gloated with satisfaction. This time it had not been a hoax, the man from the warehouse had known what he was talking about.

No one spoke. The police ransacked the rooms in the hiding place. The eight refugees hurriedly got their clothes together. Anne packed hers in her school bag. Clothes were the only thing they were allowed to bring, everything else had to be left behind, even Anne's diary.

All their nightmares, and all their worst fears and anxieties of those countless days and nights were finally coming true. The Nazis viciously obliterated any sign of human life or warmth in the rooms. One of the only things which they overlooked, the only record of the months which had been spent there, was a book which had gotten mixed up with some other papers tossed about on the floor—Anne's diary.

The eight friends were first sent to the large camp in Holland at Westerbork, which had been constructed for the sorting out of captured Jews. Anne had never dreamed that they would leave the hiding place in this way. She had always been optimistic about their fate. Their arrest and transfer to a concentration camp had been discussed frequently during moments of weariness and uncertainty. In their minds though, they

had always refused to acknowledge the idea as a real possibility. Stunned, she set out on the same road that millions of other victims had traveled before her. She saw and felt for herself the anguish that many of the friends she had mourned for had already suffered.

At Westerbork, a multitude of unidentified prisoners were crowded together in quarters that lacked even a washbasin. There were hardly any toilets either. Stripped of their garments and reclothed in blue uniforms and wooden clogs, they were assigned to the various barracks, which measured thirty yards by ten yards. Three hundred Jews had to live in each one. Amidst that mass of humanity, stripped of all individuality, the eight friends stood out on account of their pallid faces, a result of spending two years without ever going out in the sun.

"The only thing we can do is try and be strong," was the thought that went through all of their minds. They had fallen now into the hands of evil forces. Their fates depended on the frighteningly precise and rigid mechanism of the organization for human destruction which the Nazis had implemented for production-line murder.

"We mustn't lose the strength to resist," urged Mr. Frank.

They were awakened at five each morning. The work they were forced to do was very hard and the food was scarce and bad. Anne and Peter were young and found some comfort in their friendship and their attempts to help each other. During the few breaks from work they had the two went around the camp together. Mrs. Frank was very withdrawn and never talked. She washed and rewashed the few articles of clothing the family possessed. Her family and friends stayed close by her, but no one could bring her out of herself.

On August 25 the rumor that Paris had been liberated circulated throughout the camp, and hope was rekindled. But then, on September 3, the day the Allies took Brussels, a thousand Jews were chosen to leave Westerbork. The eight friends were among this last shipment of Jews to leave Holland. They boarded a long freight train, with seventy-five people crammed into each car. They were crowded together worse than animals would have been, with no air, just a little water, and some black bread. For three days and nights the train headed towards its destination. On the third night the freight cars were opened and the prisoners heard the cold, grating voices of the SS men ordering them to get down.

"Come on, out! Get on with it!" they commanded while walking up and down the station platform, keeping a close watch on the Jews as they left the train. Floodlights illuminated the desolate scene. The vague shadows of the prisoners, weakened by the journey, hunger, and terror flitted here and there in the light. In a whisper the name of Auschwitz was passed through the crowd from the leading train cars. A chill of fear ran through the Jews as they waited in a silence broken only by the harsh commands of the guards and the barking of dogs. A clear voice could be heard announcing aloofly from the loudspeaker, "Men to the right, women to the left."

There wasn't even time to say goodbye. Pushed along like the parts of some terrible machine, the women filed off to the left and the men to the right. Anne turned her head to say goodbye to her father and Peter, but it was too late. They had already been carried off into the darkness by the crowd of people shuffling along. She took Margot's hand and squeezed it tightly. Margot was looking after their mother, who by now had lost all heart.

The women walked along in the dark. The pain of separation, their weariness, and

their anxiety about their fate caused them indescribable suffering. They arrived at Block 29 of the camp at Auschwitz-Birkenau. Anne, Margot, and their mother were assigned to the same barrack house.

They soon came to know the camp at Auschwitz. It was surrounded by an electrified barbed-wire fence, which was interrupted regularly by sentry towers. In them guards with machine guns kept watch over the camp and its unfortunate inhabitants. There were never-ending rows of brick-built "blocks" for Poles, Jews, Gypsies, and Russian prisoners of war. At the main entrance to the camp there was a notice which read "ARBEIT MACHT FREI"—work will make you free.

The new arrivals had been welcomed by one of the camp's officers, "I warn you that you have not come to a hospital, but to a German concentration camp, which you will never leave except as smoke from the chimney. If you don't like it, it would be better to throw yourselves into the electrified fences."

The SS Commandant, Rudolf Franz Ferdinand Hess, assisted by members of the SS and a staff chosen from common criminals, had made Auschwitz into a model camp. The destruction of its inmates had been scientifically organized. It consisted of a grisly sequence of work, starvation, a variety of punishments and forms of torture, and death by gassing.

Anne entered into the life of the camp. Her personal possessions were confiscated and she was assigned a number which was tattooed on her arm. With almost all her hair shaved off and her thin body dressed in a gray, sack-like garment which served as her only clothing, she seemed even younger than she was. A yellow strip on a triangle was sewn onto this garment in order to distinguish her as a Jew from the other inmates there.

She soon realized that it had been a subtle form of cruelty to leave mother and daughters together. Watching each other's suffering only added to their own suffering. Nevertheless, Anne tried to turn this to good advantage using whatever means she could. Her big eyes were still able to smile.

"It will all end someday, mother, you'll see. We'll get out of here."

She went around the camp secretly and always tried to find something useful—a piece of material to cover her mother with, or some water to relieve the thirst of the infernal place.

"Drink, mother, drink."

But her mother refused, "You drink. I've already had some." Anne helped her drink, as if she were a child.

When Margot put her lips to the cup, she, too, drank like a child who had to be made to do it. Mrs. Frank, both physically and mentally, was giving up.

"We must be strong," Anne urged her sister and mother. "Daddy said we must never give in."

One day, while returning to her barracks, Anne saw a group of Hungarian children sitting in the rain waiting their turn to enter the gas chambers, she could control herself no longer.

"It's not fair! It's not fair!"

She stopped and looked in their eyes. She would have liked to save them from death, but could only weep uncontrollably at their fate, making no attempt to hide her grief.

Saying Farewell in the Camp

It will never be possible to undo the pain and horror that people endured in those concentration camps. People suffered in the worst ways that the human imagination could devise—inhuman, exhausting marches in the freezing cold and rain; roll-calls day and night; starvation; and constant fear of punishment and torture. All the while they could smell the smoke from the bodies of the people who had been put to death every day, loaded systematically onto a belt which carried them, without stopping, to the crematorium. The air was foul with the smell of burning flesh. There were no exceptions—men, women, and children either met their end that way, or in the gas chamber. Mothers' attempts to hide their young ones were in vain. Even little babies were sought out.

Auschwitz was notorious for its punishments. They were handed out publicly when the evening roll-call was made, using a leather whip on the bare skin. The idea was to provide an example for those who had to watch. Another form of punishment was standing at attention for hours or holding a heavy stone with outstretched arms for hours while kneeling. There were also the "Stehzelle". These were tiny cells where the victim had to stand up all the time, with a low door like a dog kennel. To remain there as the prisoner did, without food or water must have been an incredible torture. Sadly the only way to escape any of these horrors was to commit suicide on the electrified barbed-wire fence or be fired at by the sentries.

Anne came to know this world, and yet she continued to be strong, to fight for her life, and to provide comfort to those around her. Seeing her mother so depressed and ill caused her more pain than anything.

"Poor mother!" she often said to Margot. "There is just nothing we can do to help her."

Nearly two months had passed, when one evening in October, the youngest and strongest prisoners were selected to be transferred to another camp, Bergen-Belsen located in Germany. The news circulated among the prisoners and caused great agitation. The guards made the women leave their barracks to be checked over. While lining up, they all adjusted their clothing, and tidied their hair, attempting to improve their appearances so as to hide any signs of tiredness or weakness. Anyone who was ill, old, or weak would be rejected. One by one the women were forced to pass under a spotlight so that their conditions could be assessed. As Anne and Margot passed through a voice said, "This one, yes. This one, yes." They went and stood in another line, waiting for their mother to join them. Instead though, they heard, "This one, no."

Their mother was desperate. "For the love of God, not my children! Not my children! Don't take my children away from me!" She was overcome with grief and desperation. They were barely able to touch hands, before they said goodbye forever.

The journey to Bergen-Belsen was long. Anne and Margot were unable to speak—their capacity for hope had been tried too far. Bergen-Belsen was in Northern Germany on the road from Kiel to Hamburg. The camp was under the command of Joseph Kramer, who had come from Auschwitz. As with all the camps, his assistants were members of the SS and common criminals taken from the prisons. There were no gas chambers at this camp, and it lacked the organization found at Auschwitz, but the prisoners died

by the thousands just the same. Their deaths were caused by starvation and diseases like typhus brought about by the lack of water and sanitation. Wherever one looked there was indescribable filth. The barracks were full of ill, starving, and dying people, and the sight was truly horrifying. The living, the dying, and the dead were mingled together in abominable stench. Outside one barrack-house there was a pile of corpses, barely covered with a sprinkling of earth and lime.

Anne and Margot held each other's hands to give each other courage. "We mustn't give in!" Anne's hands seemed to say. But they both knew that it was becoming more and more difficult to go on. There was no roll-call at Bergen-Belsen, and no regular distribution of food. It was like being thrown into hell.

"Perhaps it's just another method of extermination," thought Margot. The vast number of communal graves around the camp seemed to prove that it was so.

"My friend, Lies is here at Bergen-Belsen!" said Anne, remembering what Elli had told her. In fact, Lies Goosens, Anne's dear school friend, had learned that some Dutch prisoners had arrived at the camp.

One day, through another prisoner, Anne received a message from her friend arranging a meeting. Lies was in another block, but with care it would be possible to avoid detection and meet at the fence during the evening. Anne was anxiously happy. It was dark when she left the barracks and there was an icy wind blowing. She managed to get to the prearranged place and called out quietly to her old friend.

"Lies! Lies! Where are you?"

"Anne, Anne, oh Anne! I'm here, I'm right over here!" Lies cried out, running in the direction from which Anne's voice had come.

The girls looked quite different than they had when they were schoolmates. The suffering they had endured had changed the girls' appearances greatly, making them look very thin, pale, and drawn. Their eyes met in the darkness, and the two recognized each other immediately. They spoke of themselves, their families, and their experiences quickly. How distant and unreal their time together at the Montessori school seemed now! They wept over the terrible things that had happened to them and their families. Soon though, their visit was over and it was time for them to part and return to their blocks.

"Goodbye Anne," said Lies sadly.

"See you soon, Lies!"

"Oh yes, I hope so!" Lies said as Anne began to walk away. "Anne wait, don't go just yet. I received a package from the Red Cross. I've brought you some things from it. Watch out! I'm going to throw over a sweater, a biscuit, and a little sugar for you."

"Thank you, Lies."

"Watch out! I'm throwing it over now."

Anne stood on her tip toes with her hands on the fence. There were sounds of a scuffle and after a moment's silence a despairing cry.

"A woman has stolen the things and she won't give them back."

"Don't cry, Anne. See you soon."

The winter at Bergen-Belsen was frighteningly severe. Hunger and thirst made life impossible. Those who had not resigned themselves to die in beds, corridors, or in the fields tried to survive by any means possible, including theft. There was no longer any sign of love or human kindness to be found in the place, and no respect for anyone. Only someone who has lived there can fully comprehend the wretchedness of the

camp. It is just impossible for any written document to do justice to what went on there.

Anne watched Margot growing thinner and paler by the day. She was drained of all energy and courage. Anne told her sister white lies to raise her spirits, brought her something to cover herself with, and went out to look for help for her.

But who was there to answer a young girl's plea for help in that wretched place? There was no sanitation, there were no latrines, the buildings were covered with filth, and typhus was raging. By February, 1945 Margot was no longer able to follow what Anne said. She was so weak she was unable to concentrate enough to listen. Margot was beginning to show signs of serious illness.

The camp had taken its toll on Anne, too. Sometimes in the evening she had dreams that took her back in time. They blotted out the images, voices, pain, and even the smell of the barracks. She was back in Amsterdam with her father, her mother, and Peter, too. She seemed to be at school, the high school, with her friends. Or else she was at home, talking with her mother or Margot. One night she dreamed that she was in a meadow full of flowers, and Moortje the cat was there, too, jumping out of a bush. They ran along and jumped together. The weather was so clear that you could see the sea...

Never Forget! It Must Never Happen Again

Suddenly the dream changed, and she was on the crowded Prinsengracht in Amsterdam. There was a boat in flames on the canal and there was such a foul smell in the air that she woke up with a start. It was the stench of the barracks that had disturbed her happy dreams. But the image of Moortje the cat was so strong that it comforted her somewhat.

She never dreamed about the hiding place—she thought about that while she was awake. She wondered about many things, among them whether her mother was still alive, and where Peter and her father were.

"They would help me to have the courage to go on," she thought. "Just what has happened to Peter?" Thinking about Peter took her back to the days spent in hiding. "They weren't such bad days after all," she reflected. "I read and studied so much. In spite of it all sometimes we even had very happy times! If only we could all still be there together, waiting for peace to come!"

Sometimes, when she threw herself down in exhaustion on her bed, she almost wanted to die, but then, the thought that she just had to keep on living for the sake of her loved ones gave her fresh strength. She had to survive to tell the people of the world of the suffering she had known so that no one would ever forget what had happened.

As determined as she was, Anne was still unable to survive the horrors of Bergen-Belsen. In March of 1945, just a few days after her sister's death, Anne also died. Two months later the war came to an end.

Anne's Diary

Germany was defeated in the spring of 1945 and the war was over. In the event of defeat the Nazis had made plans for the destruction of the concentration camps, and the elimination of those who were still alive in them. They wanted to hide from the world the horrors they had perpetrated there, especially in the death camps.

The Allied advance had taken the Nazis by surprise on all fronts. Because of this their plans to destroy the camps and the evidence of their cruelty had only been partially carried out.

When the gates of the camps were thrown open the world learned, much to its horror, of the dreadful treatment that millions of innocent victims had been subjected to and of the horrendous way so many had died. The camps, the cells, the ovens, the graves, the walls, the ground—wherever one looked there was evidence of the most terrifying methods for torture and death ever devised on earth.

In January, 1945, while the sound of the Russian guns was echoing in Poland, where Auschwitz was, the SS had heard rumors that the Russian army might liberate the prisoners. It was decided that immediately, eleven thousand Jews had to be moved on foot to other death camps located in Germany. Otto Frank was in the hospital at the Auschwitz concentration camp and remained there simply because no one ever sent for him. During that never-ending march to Germany nearly all of the Jews died of fatigue, hunger, or cold.

As soon as the Russians arrived, Mr. Frank was taken to Kattowicze and from there to Odessa. Finally, he was able to return to Holland by ship from Marseilles.

Otto Frank was the sole survivor of the eight who had lived in the hiding place. After the war he was reunited with Mr. Kraler and Mr. Koophuis, and the others who had helped him, his family, and friends during the many months they had spent hiding from the Nazis. There was so much to talk about.

"How often I thought about you," said Mr. Frank, overcome with emotion. "You all could have died helping us as you did."

We have never regretted what we did," one of them said. The others all nodded their heads and murmured in agreement.

"Mr. Frank," said Elli, "we have something for you. Miep, why don't you give it to him?"

Miep handed him a book, "We found it in the hiding place. It had been abandoned with all the papers that were scattered about after the Gestapo had finished searching the place."

"It's Anne's diary, it's my little girl's diary! I can't believe it!" he exclaimed. More than that he was unable to say. Words failed him. Emotions and memories churned inside him. He held the little book, remembering just how much it had meant to his young daughter.

Later, when Otto Frank was alone he took out Anne's diary. "I don't want to invade your privacy or expose your secret feelings," he thought to himself as he opened the book, "I just want to be with you for awhile, to remember you as you were, and read what you have written."

On the first page, Anne had written:

"I hope that I will be able to confide in you as I never confided in anyone else, and I hope that you will be a great strength to me. Anne Frank. June 12, 1942."

The words on the pages were priceless to him, "Thank God it wasn't lost," he said, and hugged the book to his chest. He looked at the book, thumbing through it and reading passages at random. He found that Anne had written down many things about herself and her feelings. She described their life together in the secret hiding place, putting down her many observations about how difficult it was to be understood, about the food, the thieves, the Van Daans, about Dussel, about everyone and everything.

"To give me and Margot a present, Daddy has emptied one of the filing cabinets in the offices and filled it with filing cards. It's going to be a catalogue of books. We are both going to write down the names of the books we've read, their authors and summaries of the plots. We can also write down what we thought of each book. I've got myself another exercise book for foreign words."

"They were so clever, those two, so busy and serious!" Mr. Frank recalled. "Can they still be alive?" he hoped. "I wonder where they were taken after we were separated at Auschwitz? Where could they be now?"

"Yesterday evening," wrote Anne on March 10, "There was a short circuit, and the shooting went on and on outside. I thought it would never end. I can never get over my fear of the shooting and the roar of the planes flying overhead dropping bombs and making the earth shake so. I creep into father's bed nearly every night for comfort. I suppose it's very childish of me, but it makes me feel so much safer."

"I was afraid, too," her father admitted to himself, "but I tried to behave like a brave soldier to reassure you."

"Spinach and salad for fourteen days now. Sweet potatoes ten inches long that taste moldy. Things have come to a pretty pass..."

It was almost as if he could hear her laughing about her threadbare slippers, about the condition of her mother's and Margot's blouses, and her own, which was so short that her tummy was left uncovered.

"The poetry Daddy wrote for me on my birthday is so beautiful that I'm not going to share it with you."

"She was fourteen years old when she wrote this." he reflected, "Just fourteen years old and she was so happy with a poem or a book about Roman and Greek myths." He couldn't read the diary entries in order. Instead, he jumped backwards and forwards over the days and months.

"I wander from room to room and up and down the stairs. I feel like a little bird that has been cruelly deprived of its wings. 'Get out into the fresh air, and laugh!' a voice cries inside me."

Anne's writing was so touching and stirred so many memories in him that his distress got the better of him, and he moved ahead to the last page.

"I know exactly what I would like to be and what I am inside, but alas, I am like that only with myself!"

"Not any more," he said to himself. "Now everyone will know who you are, my little Anne!"

On May 22, 1944, Anne had written:

"I love Holland, I once hoped, and I still do hope, that Holland can be a homeland for me, a person without a country. Even though I was born in Germany I have lived in this country so long that it has become more a home to me than my real homeland."

In a certain way her hope was fulfilled. Even though she had returned to the earth, Holland remained her adopted country. The Queen of the Netherlands received her father and conferred a high honor on him in direct recognition of the little writer who had made known the dramatic plight of the Jews, and also the plight of wartime Holland, occupied and humiliated by invading forces.

Anne had also written in her diary:

"I want to live on after I have died. I am glad, then, that God has given me the desire to write down everything about myself... I must, I must, I must..."

Anne's desire was so strong, and she had expressed it so movingly, that her father felt it as he read her diary. He took it upon himself to fulfill her wish. After her death the diary was published and she did become a famous writer. Through the actions of Otto Frank and his friends, her diary was first published by Contact Publishers in Amsterdam in June, 1947, and called "The Secret Annexe". Perhaps even then they did not quite realize the true value of the extraordinary document. Written by anyone it would have been an important, realistic account of the day to day life and anxieties of a Jew living in Nazi-occupied Holland. But it was even more extraordinary because it had been written by an adolescent girl.

The diary is now well-known throughout the world and it has been translated into many languages, including Arabic and Chinese! Without any exaggeration it can be said that millions of people have been and still are moved by the story of her family's plight at the hands of the Nazis and the fate of the Jews. They take Anne's messages about peace and humanity into their hearts.

After the war Otto Frank settled permanently in Amsterdam. He spent the rest of his life working endlessly to ensure that the suffering from the war and the persecution of the Jews would not be forgotten or repeated. The city of Amsterdam assured him that the reconstruction program to rebuild the city after the war would intentionally leave the warehouse with the secret hiding place intact. It would serve as a permanent reminder of the terrible affair.

Thus, Number 263 on the Prinsengracht was completely restored. It is maintained by the Anne Frank Foundation, a youth center run by young people with the aim of working for peace and progess in the world, as Anne had always dreamed.

The Frank's hiding place is exactly as it was when Anne wrote her diary. The stairways still lead up to the dark old rooms with their clumsy furniture and faded carpets. A visit there is a very moving experience, any other people present seem to fade away, and one is left alone with Anne's memory. Above all else, aside from the final images of that tragic August, the concentration camp, and her sacrifices, we are left with the insights of a young girl who grew up with pain and suffering, and who can yet teach us something of the love of life.

The Secret Hiding Place

The building of Kohlen & Co. is located at No. 263 on the Prinsengracht Canal in Amsterdam. On the ground floor is a large warehouse with the offices located on the first floor. The secret rooms where the eight refugees lived are on the second and third floors. A wooden staircase led from the first-floor corridor to the second-floor landing where there were two doors. The one on the left led to the street, storeroom, and the attics from where a steep staircase led down to the second street door.

The right-hand door led to the internal flat where the hiding place was. No one suspected that so many rooms lay concealed behind an ordinary gray door. Immediately upon entering there was a steep staircase on the right, and on the left a short corridor which led to the bedroom belonging to Anne's parents. A small adjoining room belonged to the Franks' daughters, Anne and Margot. On the right of the staircase there was a small, windowless room with a washbasin and separate toilet. There was a communication door between this room and the sisters' room.

Upon opening the door at the top of the stairs, one was astonished to find such a large, well-lit room in an old house on the canal. There was a gas oven (thanks to the fact that the room had once been a laboratory) and a sink. The room doubled as a kitchen and the Van Daan's bedroom, as well as being the dining room, living room, and work room for all the refugees.

A small hallway became Peter's apartment. Then, finally, as on the street side of the rest of the building, there was an attic.

This model of the secret lodgings can be seen at the Anne Frank Foundation. The Foundation maintains the building at 263 Prinsengracht, where eight people lived in hiding for two years and one month.

House Rules in the Hideway

This is a humorous entry from Anne's diary which she described as a "Prospectus and Guide to the 'Secret Annexe' ".

Open all year round Beautiful, quiet, free from woodland surroundings, in the heart of Amsterdam. Can be reached by trams 13 and 17, also by car or bicycle. In special cases also on foot, if the Germans prevent the use of transport.

Board and lodging: Free.

Special fat-free diet.

Running water in the bathroom (alas, no bath) and down various inside and outside walls.

Ample storage room for all types of goods.

Own radio center, direct communication with London, New York, Tel Aviv, and numerous other stations. This appliance is only for residents' use after six o'clock in the evening. No stations are forbidden, on the understanding that German stations are only listened to in special cases, such as classical music and the like.

Rest hours: 10 o'clock in the evening until 7:30 in the morning. 10:15 on Sundays. Residents may rest during the day, conditions permitting, as the director indicates. For reasons of public security rest hours must be strictly observed!!

Holidays (outside the home): postponed indefinitely.

Use of language: Speak softly at all times, by order! All civilized languages are permitted, therefore no German!

Lessons: One written shorthand lesson per week. English, French, Mathematics, and History at all times.

Small Pets-Special Department (permit is necessary): Good treatment available (vermin excepted).

Mealtimes: breakfast, every day except Sunday and Bank Holidays, 9 am. Sundays and Bank Holidays, 11:30 am approximately.

Lunch: (not very big): 1:15 pm to 1:45 pm.

Dinner: cold and/or hot: no fixed time (depending on the news broadcast).

Duties: Residents must always be ready to help with office work.

Baths: The washtub is available for all residents from 9 am on Sundays. The W.C., kitchen, private office, or main office, whichever preferred, are available.

Alcoholic Beverages: only with doctor's prescription.

The end

Letters from Anne's Diary

Monday, 22 May, 1944

...To our great horror and regret we hear that the attitude of a great many people towards us Jews has changed. We hear that there is anti-Semitism now in circles that never thought of it before. The news has affected us all very, very deeply. The cause of this hatred of the Jews is understandable, even human sometimes, but not good. The Christians blame the Jews for giving secrets away to the Germans, for betraying their helpers and for the fact that, through the Jews a great many Christians have gone the way of so many others before them, and suffered terrible punishments and a dreadful fate...

When one hears this one naturally wonders why we are carrying on with this long and difficult war. We always hear that we're all fighting together for freedom, truth, and right!...

Tuesday, 6 June, 1944

Great commotion in the "Secret Annexe"! Would the long awaited liberation that has been talked of so much, but which still seems too wonderful, too much like a fairy tale, ever come true? Could we be granted victory this year, 1944? We don't know yet, but hope is revived within us; it gives us fresh courage, and makes us strong again. Since we must put up bravely with all the fears, privations, and sufferings, the great thing now is to remain calm and steadfast. Now more than ever we must clench our teeth and not cry out. France, Russia, Italy, and Germany, too, can all cry out and give vent to their misery, but we haven't the right to do that yet!... Oh, Kitty, the best part of the invasion is that I have the feeling that friends are approaching. We have been oppressed by those terrible Germans for so long, they have had their knives so at our throats, that the thoughts of friends and delivery fills us with confidence!

Thursday, 15 June, 1944

I wonder if it's because I haven't been able to poke my nose outdoors for so long that I've grown so crazy about everything to do with nature? I can perfectly well remember that there was a time when a deep blue sky, the song of the birds, moonlight and flowers could never have kept me spellbound. That's changed since I've been here.

...A lot of people are fond of nature, many sleep outdoors occasionally, and people in prisons and hospitals long for the day when they will be free to enjoy the beauties of nature, but few are so shut away and isolated from that which can be shared alike by rich and poor. It's not imagination on my part when I say that to look up at the sky, the clouds, the moon, and the stars makes me calm and patient.... Mother Nature makes me humble and prepared to face every blow courageously.

The roof and small attic room of the hideaway. From this window the refugees could see the outside world, but only at night when there was no risk of being seen.

Anne's Concentration Camps

1. WESTERBORK (Holland)

Reuter, head of the SS in occupied Holland, wrote the following account to Himmler, head of the Reich police force, in 1942:

At last I can give you a report on the elimination of the Jews. So far we have sent twenty thousand Jews to Mauthausen and Auschwitz. There are about a hundred and twenty thousand still alive in Holland. We have established a work camp at Westerbork to which the Jews go willingly because they live and work there relatively peacefully. We haven't interfered up to now so that the greatest possible number of Jews will seek refuge there on their own accord. Many of them are still in contact with their relatives—about twenty thousand of them. I will have the relatives arrested October 1st—we know exactly where they are living. This will mean another thirty thousand people who, together with those already mentioned, will enable us to reduce by half the number of Dutch Jews by Christmas.

2. AUSCHWITZ (Poland)

The Germans established the Auschwitz Concentration Camp where ten thousand people at a time went to the gas chambers and, according to the estimate of the camp commandant himself, no less than three million people were murdered in one way or another. Auschwitz was first built to eliminate Polish resistance fighters and then the whole unhappy population of Poland. In 1941 Himmler gave orders for it to be expanded and for the surrounding marshes to be drained. The new camp was called Birkenau and it was put to immediate use for over a hundred thousand Russian prisoners. The first Jews arrived from Silesia and Slovakia. From the very beginning the disabled were gassed in a room at the crematorium... In the same year Hess was given responsibility for "the final solution".

Auschwitz was considered the most suitable camp for the physical elimination of the Jews by using gas. We have it from the commandant of the camp himself, the notorious Rudolf Hess, that more than seventy thousand Russian prisoners were put to death there. He himself states that the Germans put to death no less than ten thousand deported Jews a day. It is recorded that the death trains which arrived regularly at Auschwitz contained ninety thousand people from Slovakia, sixty-five thousand from Greece, eleven thousand from France, twenty thousand from Belgium, ninety thousand from Holland, four hundred thousand from Hungary, two hundred and fifty thousand from Poland and upper Silesia, and a hundred thousand from Germany.

Adapted from "The Scourge of the Swastika", Lord Russell of Liverpool

3. BERGEN-BELSEN (Germany)

This camp was situated near the village of Bergen on the Kiel-Hamburg road. Under the direction of an expert from Auschwitz, the camp was designed to take in the diseased and sick from the various concentration camps and factories and farms, as well as those deported from northwest Europe. When he entered the camp, the leader of the British troops, General Hughes, found it impossible to describe the conditions in the camp.

"No description can possibly give an idea of the horrors we saw outside the barracks, and inside the scene was even more terrible. There were piles of corpses inside and outside the barrack buildings—piles which also contained people still alive. At the crematorium there were mounds of corpses waiting to be covered over located next to other newly-filled communal graves... The barracks were packed with prisoners, sick and starved beyond belief. In some buildings, intended for a hundred people, there were up to a thousand inmates!"

Historical Chronology

Anne's Life	Historical and Cultural Events
1933 The Frank family moves to Amsterdam, Holland, to escape Nazi persecution brought about by Hitler's racist laws.	**1933** January 30—Nazis win power in Germany under Hitler.
	1933/ 1935 Hitler establishes a Nazi dictatorship in Germany, the Third Reich. He dissolves parliament and abolishes all constitutional rights. All political parties and trade unions are abolished. The political police force, called the Gestapo, is founded, and concentration camps for the elimination of opposition are opened.
1935 Anne Frank begins attending the Montessori school.	**1934** August—Hitler assumes full powers: he becomes head of state, Chancellor of the Reich, and head of the armed forces. He adopts the title of Fuhrer. He establishes as state doctrine the principle of Arian racial superiority, commences the persecution of the Jews, and imposes obligatory conscription and rearmament.
	1935/ 1936 Attack on, and conquest of, Ethiopia by fascist Italy.

Frankfurt—Romer Square with its typical medieval atmosphere.

Amsterdam—A view from the air showing the canals and the Mondelbaan tower.

Berlin—The Brandenburg Gate decorated with Swastikas.

The identification mark which all the Jews were required to wear on their clothing.

Anne's Life	Historical and Cultural Events
	1936/ 1939 Civil war in Spain. Nazi-Fascist intervention in support of Franco. The Berlin-Rome military Alliance.
	1938 Hitler annexes Austria.
1939 The Dutch government proclaims its neutrality.	**1939** The Germans occupy Czechoslovakia. September 1—The Germans invade Poland. France and Britain declare war on Germany. The Second World War begins.
1940 Motorized German troops and parachutists occupy strategic points in Holland. Bombing of the large cities begins. The Dutch Queen and the government take refuge in London.	**1940** April 9—Germany invades Denmark and Norway. May 10—Germany invades Holland, Belgium, and Luxembourg. June 10—Italy joins Germany. June 22—The collapse and surrender of France. De Gaulle organizes French anti-Nazi resistance.
1941 The special Nazi laws are extended to Holland. Anne Frank is obliged to leave the Montessori school and enroll in a Jewish school. February 25-26—The people of Amsterdam strike in protest against abuse directed at the Jews.	**1941** The Germans go on to invade Rumania, Bulgaria, and Greece. June 22—Germany attacks the Soviet Union. The war escalates.

Guernica, Painted by Pablo Picasso as a protest against Nazi involvement in Spain.

A photograph of the Warsaw ghetto. Attempts to exit from the ghetto were punished with death.

Norway was occupied by the Germans. This photograph shows German troops at Tromso.

The first day of the invasion of Russia. Armored German troops in the Ukraine.

Anne's Life	Historical and Cultural Events
	1941 December 7—The Japanese attack the American fleet at Pearl Harbor in the Hawaiian Islands. The United States is obliged to enter the war. The war spreads to Asia and Africa.
1942 June 12—Anne is given her "diary" as a birthday gift and starts to write it in letter form. The letters are written to an imaginary friend, Kitty. July 6—Anne Frank takes refuge with her family in a secret hiding place in the building where her father works.	**1942** December—The Russians stop the Germans at Moscow.
1942/ 1944 Dutch resistance fighters intensify their activity and Nazi repressive measures are increased—capital punishment, mass deportation, forced recruitment of labor.	
	1943 January/February—The Nazis capitulate at Stalingrad. July—The Allies land in Sicily. July 25—Fascism is overthrown in Italy. September 8—Italy asks for an armistice with the United States and England and is occupied by the Germans. Mussolini establishes the Salo Republic.

Pearl Harbor—the wreck of a sunken naval unit which has become a national monument.

A page of the manuscript of Anne Frank's diary, addressed to her imaginary friend Kitty.

A 1944 poster—"The blood of thousands of Poles will be avenged in battle".

The first winter of the Russian campaign. German troops begin to lose heart.

Anne's Life	Historical and Cultural Events
1944 August 4—Acting upon information provided by an informer, a Gestapo officer discovers the hiding place. The eight Jews are arrested. Early August—Anne Frank is sent with her family to Westerbork, a transit camp for Jews. September 2—Anne is moved with her family to Auschwitz (Poland) where she is separated from her father. October 30—Anne and Margot, now separated from their mother, are put on board a train of young prisoners headed for the concentration camp of Bergen-Belsen (Germany). November 9—Southern Holland is liberated by the first Allied offensive.	**1944** June 6—The Allies land in Normandy.
	1944/ 1945 The Russians and the Allies make major progress in rolling back the German forces on both the Eastern and Western Fronts.
1945 February—Anne and Margot succumb to typhus. March—Anne dies shortly after her sister and is buried in a communal grave at Bergen-Belsen. April—Holland is liberated.	**1945** April 25—The Liberation of Italy. May 2—Hitler commits suicide May 8—Germany surrenders. The war ends in Europe. August 6-9—The Americans drop two atomic bombs on Japan.

Paris—The parade of liberation troops along the Champs-Elysées.

Berlin—June 1945: Zukov, Montgomery, and Rokossosvkij.

Amsterdam—The building where the "Secret Annexe" was, which now houses the Anne Frank Foundation.

Books for Further Reading

Prisoners of War by Ronald Bailey,
Time-Life Books, 1981.

Anne Frank: The Diary of a Young Girl by Anne Frank,
translated by B.M. Mooyaart, Pocket Books, 1953.

Secret Armies: Resistance Groups in World War Two
by Tim Healy, Silver Burdett, 1981.

The Wall by John Hersey,
Bantam Books, 1981.

The Nazis by Robert Herzstein,
Time-Life Books, 1979.

2 3 4 5 6 7 8 9 10—IL—93 92 91 90 89 88 87 86